The Great

Tiki DRINK

Book

The Great Tiki DRINK Book

JENNIFER
TRAINER THOMPSON
with Nancy Thomas

TEN SPEED PRESS
Berkeley | Toronto

Ten Speed Press
Box 7123
Berkeley, California 94707
www.tenspeed.com

Distributed in Australia by Simon & Schuster Australia, in Canada by Ten Speed Press Canada, in New Zealand by Southern Publishers Group, in South Africa by Real Books, and in the United Kingdom and Europe by Airlift Book Company.

Cover and interior design by Toni Tajima
Photographs on pages ii, 23, 26–27, 49, 50, 53, 54, 57, 60
    by Kristen Brochmann © Ronnie Sellers Productions
Photographs on pages v, vi, 2, 3, 12, 18, 25, 30, 31, 34, 35, 36, 37, 38, 40, 43, 47, 48, 52, 61, 64, 67, 72, 77, 79, 84, 86, 88, 90–91, 92, 104 by Kevin Kennefick © Ronnie Sellers Productions
Photograph on page 8–9 © by Scott Lindgren
Images on pages 7, 32, and 33 courtesy of Retroactive
    Publishing Services, Inc. www.retroactive.com
Illustrations and photographs on pages viii, 4, 5, 6, 10–11, 16, 23, 28–29, 45, 46, 62, 96, graciously provided from the archives of Trader Vic's.

Library of Congress Cataloging-in-Publication Data
Thompson, Jennifer Trainer.
  The great tiki drink book / Jennifer Trainer Thompson with Nancy Thomas.
      p. cm.
Includes index.
  ISBN 1-58008-405-2
  1. Cocktails. 2. Cookery, Polynesian. 3. Menus. I. Thomas, Nancy. II. Title.
  TX951 .T484 2002
  641.8′74–dc21   2001008227

First printing, 2002
Printed in China

4 5 6 7 8 9 10 – 07 06 05 04 03

Contents

Introduction / 1

Cocktails / 17

Appetizers / 63

Menu Suggestions / 93

Resources / 95

Index / 100

About the Author / 104

Acknowledgments

I live in a sleepy New England college town, where I suspect there are more cows than people. Several years ago, the scene changed considerably when Nancy Thomas (who has a curious blend of Oklahoman and Moroccan roots) opened Mezze, a tiny, sleek restaurant that offered a delectable grazing menu (*mezze* are little dishes found throughout the Mediterranean). People flocked from miles around, and several years later she opened Eleven, a vibrant bistro tucked into a nineteenth-century building at MASS MoCA, an electronics factory turned contemporary art museum in nearby North Adams. Nancy and her staff serve great food, and I learned more recently that she's also an inspired mixologist, as evinced by her collaboration on many of the drinks and appetizers on the following pages. (And she cheerfully endured my mantra: "not too sweet!") Thank you, Nancy.

I'd also like to thank others who helped with this book and the associated photo shoots: photographers Kristen Brochmann and Kevin Kennefick, Jody Fijal, Franklin Eck, Omar Montoya, Brian Antoni, Ed Batres, Lee Mylks, Kristen Cummings, Carolyn Beaudreau, Judy Huber, Jim and Mary Jane Thompson, and David McFate. Thanks to my editor, Annie Nelson. A special thanks to Trader Vic's for generously lending archival materials used in this book. Thanks also to Eziba, Skidoo, and Duffy's Love Shack for the loan of some wonderfully whimsical objects. And my hat's off to Sven Kirsten, author of *The Book of Tiki*, the definitive book about this curious slice of American culture.

Introduction

Even at the finest bars, most drinks are served up barely noticed. What can you say about a clear gin and tonic, other than that it's cold and nicely astringent? But tiki, that rollicking Auntie Mame, demands to be noticed as she lands at your table, flowering or in flames. A tiki drink isn't just a cocktail, it's an attitude.

Why? First are the tiki drink's flamboyant looks. One can't ignore a drink that arrives festooned with Day-Glo monkeys, rainbow-colored parrots, and tiny paper umbrellas. In living color, reminiscent of the shallow waters off Virgin Gorda on a cloudless day (or, if it's a bit off, a glass of Windex), a tiki drink takes presentation to a whopping new dimension. Even the container is emphasized, ranging from a sultry ceramic hula girl glass to a tacky tiki god mug the size of a salad bowl.

Nor can you ignore the charismatic names. Most drink names are prosaic by default: rum and Coke, Seven and Seven, scotch and soda. The names of tiki drinks are sheer poetry, conjuring up the glory age of cocktails (with its Manhattans and old-fashioneds) steered left of center by Polynesian fantasies. Who can resist the Suffering Bastard or not be intrigued by a Missionary's Downfall? Even if you've never been to the Raffles Hotel, a Singapore Sling can transport you there, circa 1890, conjuring Brits lounging in colonial splendor in oversized wicker chairs under hypnotizing ceiling fans, absorbing both the withering heat and the ensuing relief of a tropical libation.

But the most delightful and satisfying aspect of a tiki drink is the taste. If a tiki drink is made poorly (and, regrettably, many have been), it can be sickly sweet and cloying.

But if it is made correctly, there is an exquisite tension between sour and sweet, not to mention between strong ingredients such as rum and "weak" flavors such as coconut, vanilla, or freshly grated nutmeg. I defy you to sip Nancy's Grass Skirt without begging for another.

Tiki drinks are a refreshing way to thwart the sweltering heat of a summer afternoon or evening. They are great for outdoor parties, and, as you'll find in this book, some are even delightful sipping drinks for late nights in the dead of winter by a roaring fire. Paired with spicy foods, tiki drinks are perfect foils to chile-laced Asian and island dishes, such as Thai Curry Spring Rolls with Spicy Mango-Apricot Sauce (page 66 and page 89).

Tiki Pop: Where It Began

The name *tiki* derives from the Polynesian god Tiki, who the Polynesians considered to be the First Man. (The fact that *tiki* is also an affectionate term in the islands for a man's sex organ—*tiki-poto* is the female counterpart—is an indication of the light-heartedness with which this god has been worshiped.) Tiki is also the name of the carved stone and wooden statues of tiki gods that are found everywhere from Hawaii to Easter Island to New Zealand.

For centuries, Europeans and North Americans have idealized the garden of Eden–like qualities of the Polynesian islands. Many artists at the turn of the century, such as Picasso, Gauguin, and Miró, were inspired by primitivism, and Picasso even bought a tiki from the Marquesas Islands in 1910 that he kept with him his entire life. In 1915, Hawaiian-style guitar playing and hula dancers were featured at San Francisco's Panama-Pacific International Exhibition, and Americans went wild over ukuleles and the exotic music, beginning a Hawaiian music rage that swept the United States and England. In 1916, the Victor Record Company (which later became RCA Victor) sold more Hawaiian records than any other style of music.

But it wasn't until the repeal of Prohibition in 1933 that two Californians, at opposite ends of the state, helped nudge the Polynesian drink craze into motion. One was a wily former bootlegger named Ernest Beaumont-Gantt, who in 1934 put up palm trees at a roadside joint in Hollywood and called it Don the Beachcomber. Heavy on style—with Hawaiian-jungle décor, hula girl waitresses, and expert drinks served creatively (some in whole pineapples)—Don the Beachcomber became a happening place for the Hollywood film industry. Beaumont-Gantt served mostly rum (it was cheaper than

whiskey and gin in those days) and, to counter its cheap "rummy" reputation, mixed it with exotic ingredients and gave the drinks inspired names such as Test Pilot, Three Dots and a Dash, and his most famous, the Zombie, which was served at the 1939 New York World's Fair. Buoyed by success, Beaumont-Gantt changed his name to Donn Beach and with his wife franchised the operation from Chicago to Hawaii.

Meanwhile, up the coast in Oakland, a gourmand named Victor Bergeron opened a hunting camp–style bar (think deer heads and snowshoes) called Hinky Dinks in 1934.

A serious foodie who took bartending just as seriously, Bergeron traveled the world studying drinks, from the Ritz bar in Paris to funky dirt-floored bars in Cuba. His travels took him to Don the Beachcomber's, the success of whose escapist Polynesian theme during the Great Depression inspired Bergeron to switch Hinky Dinks' décor to a tropical island motif, with carved wooden tikis at the entrance, and to change the name to Trader Vic's. He was a brilliant marketer. Over the next few decades, Bergeron built an international restaurant empire with Trader Vic's and mainstreamed Polynesian-inspired drinking and eating in the process.

Both men were in the right place at the right time, and they were talented enough to capitalize on the South Seas

HINKY DINKS: OAKLAND, CALIFORNIA

tidal wave that swept middle-class America at the end of World War II, when soldiers hurried home from the South Pacific with tales of azure blue lagoons, lush trees bearing strange sweet fruit, and women wearing clothes made of grass and feathers. Middle-class America heard Bali Hai calling in the 1950s, and Polynesian style flourished and penetrated the pop culture through the early 1970s, in everything from

VICTOR "TRADER VIC" BERGERON

5

TRADER VIC'S RESTAURANT

books (Thor Heyerdahl's *Kon-Tiki*, James Michener's *Hawaii*) to television (*Hawaii Five-O*, *Gilligan's Island*) to songs (Bing Crosby's first gold record was *Sweet Leilani*) to movies (Elvis in *Blue Hawaii*) and Broadway musicals (*South Pacific*).

Moreover, roadside tiki architecture started appearing across America, from bowling alleys to motels, gas stations and ski resorts—there was even a trailer park named "Bali Hai Estates." Tiki bars and icons decorated many basement rec rooms, and luau parties—replete with tiki torches, flower leis, limbo dancing, and lethal drinks—flourished in the suburbs.

But by the mid 1970s, tiki pop was out of style. With the easy availability of drugs, marijuana supplanted alcohol as a preferred substance, and as the sexual revolution began to swing, there was no need to go to a restaurant to fantasize about bikini-clad waitresses and joke about "getting lei'd." With a new focus on healthy eating, pupu platters were pooh-poohed. Minimalism gripped the art world. Jimmy Buffett inspired changes in attitude (if not latitude) by shifting the fantasy from Bali Hai to Margaritaville. Tiki—always dancing on that fine line between chic and tacky—fell from grace.

Today, tiki is back, and it's hot. Dozens of Web sites are dedicated to the burgeoning tiki revival scene. Jimmy Vaughan, Johnny Winter, and other rockers are tearing down the house

TABOO COVE: THE VENETIAN, LAS VEGAS

as they mix Hawaiian slide guitar with Delta and Chicago blues. Even Martha Stewart is trying to rock with polite tiki parties in her namesake magazine. (It's interesting to note that through the 1980s, people talked about "Polynesian style," and tiki drinks were called "Polynesian drinks." It wasn't until the tiki revival in the 1990s that "tiki style" became a common expression, and Polynesian drinks were dubbed "tiki" drinks.)

No doubt part of the mysterious rhythm of fashion and nostalgia, the tiki revival is also a tribute to the sheer good taste of a well-constructed drink. People have always loved a great cocktail, and a good tiki drink is both complex to taste and beautiful to behold. Moreover, rum is huge—not only is it the most popular distilled spirit in the world, but Americans are cottoning on to what the tropical world has known for years: that aged rums are as exquisite as single malts and are delicious mixed or just as sipping drinks. While some tiki

drinks in this book are all-out blends of tropical flavors, others emphasize the taste of the rum.

Overall, you'll find here a blend of vintage tiki libations along with new concoctions, all inspired by the spirit of tiki. And while I'm not one to criticize a dashboard hula girl, tiki needn't necessarily be kitschy or retro. I recently visited a tiki bar in New York that was sleekly decorated in a pared-down tropical style—nary a volcanic eruption, tribal totem, or thatched hut in sight. The recipes in this book are also more enlightened: instead of pupu platters, I invite you to try Tamarind-Glazed Beef (page 68) or Curry Puffs with Cilantro-Coconut Sauce (pages 80 and 90).

So get out your Demerara rum, turn on some Jimmy Vaughan, and enjoy a taste of aloha.

—Jennifer Trainer Thompson

Tiki Timeline

1910: Pablo Picasso buys a Marquesan tiki.

1915: The ukelele is introduced to American music lovers at the 1915 Pan Pacific International Expo in San Francisco.

1920s: The Hawaiian music craze sweeps North America.

1933: Repeal of Prohibition.

1934: Don the Beachcomber bar opens in Hollywood, and the Zombie is invented.

1939: The Zombie is served at the New York World's Fair.

1944: Victor "Trader Vic" Bergeron invents the Mai Tai.

1945: World War II ends; soldiers return from South Pacific.

1948: James Michener's TALES OF THE SOUTH PACIFIC wins the Pulitzer Prize.

1949: Trader Vic opens his first outpost, The Outrigger, in Seattle.

1951: KON-TIKI wins an Oscar for best documentary.

1959: HAWAIIAN EYE becomes a hit TV series.

1964: Stanley Kubrick and Bob Fosse come up with the idea of 2001: A SPACE ODYSSEY at Trader Vic's in New York.

1970s: Jimmy Buffett shifts Shangri La from Polynesia to Margaritaville.

1980s: Tiki falls from fashion.

1999: Tiki fever stages a cult comeback; tiki Web sites proliferate on the Internet.

2000: Exoticon, a convention of tiki art and exotic music, draws 1,500 people in Los Angeles.

2001: Martha Stewart features a tiki party in her magazine.

2001: Politiki (a bar in Washington, D.C.) opens.

Tips on Making a Great Tiki Drink

- Remove the ice from the freezer just before making the drink. Ice that's been left out gets watery, whereas a well-frozen cube will create a beautiful "smoking" effect when it hits the liquor, and it will keep your drink undiluted (at least for a while).

- The quality of the ingredients is key. Always use the freshest ingredients (for example, squeeze your own lime and lemon juice and make your own sour mix–there's a recipe on page 23). Line up all the ingredients in order before you begin to assemble the drink (delaying the mixing process can make a drink watery).

- Don't buy cheap booze. You can't make cheap whiskey taste like top shelf, so buy the best ingredients you can afford.

- If you can find it, icehouse ice is the best ice to use for making drinks, because it's much colder than regular ice, and it's tasteless. Icehouses used to be in every city; now you can find them in coastal cities where there is a large fishing industry, such as New Bedford (near where I hail from). Some supermarkets also package icehouse ice.

- A metal cocktail shaker comes in handy for chilling drinks. Fill a metal shaker with ice and the drink ingredients and shake vigorously until a frost appears on the shaker, about 15 seconds. If you shake too little, your drink won't be blended; if you shake too much, your drink will be watery. The goal is to get the drink cold as quickly as possible. Use plenty of ice; if using crushed ice, note that it dilutes the drink faster than cubes. There are two types of shakers, both available at popular housewares chains, as well as on online auction sites and at secondhand shops. The first is the classic three-piece cocktail shaker, which includes a container, strainer, and lid and is used to both chill and strain a drink. The second is a simple tapered stainless steel tumbler that fits on a standard rocks glass (it looks like a smaller version of the metal container used for making milk-shakes). It is useful for shaking the ingredients with the ice in the serving glass.

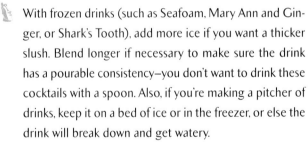 With frozen drinks (such as Seafoam, Mary Ann and Ginger, or Shark's Tooth), add more ice if you want a thicker slush. Blend longer if necessary to make sure the drink has a pourable consistency—you don't want to drink these cocktails with a spoon. Also, if you're making a pitcher of drinks, keep it on a bed of ice or in the freezer, or else the drink will break down and get watery.

Don't feel you have to put mind-bending amounts of alcohol in tiki drinks. Strive for a balance of ingredients.

If you want to experiment, there are three simple ingredients in many tiki drinks: lime, sugar, and rum. The sugar can take many forms, from tropical fruits to liqueurs. You can also use flavor enhancers such as vanilla, nutmeg, anise, or lemongrass.

Buying Rum for Tiki Drinks

Rum is a spirit distilled from cane juice or molasses, which is made from sugarcane. Rum is the number-one selling liquor in the world—it even outsells tequila in Mexico! Styles of rum include:

WHITE (OR LIGHT) RUMS: Light-bodied and clear, these rums usually have a light flavor and aroma and are popular in mixers. Be mindful that they are delicate and will get lost among strong flavors.

GOLDEN (OR AMBER) RUMS: Medium-bodied, these rums are often aged in oak barrels and sometimes have caramel coloring added. They have a smooth, mellow flavor and are good for sipping or for mixing when you want the rum flavor to emerge.

DARK RUMS: Heavy and full-flavored, these rich, caramel-tasting rums are made in pot stills and sometimes aged in well-charred barrels. Good for sipping or for mixing when you want the rum flavor to come through, they can stand up to liqueurs and fruits and work well in punches.

DEMERARA RUM: This prized dark rum, made by distillers in the county of Demerara in Guyana, often has a higher proof than others and is known for a memorably woody, almost burnt aromatic flavor. Demerara is good for sipping or for mixing in a cocktail.

AGED (AÑEJO) RUMS: Like good single malts, these are expensive, vintage rums distilled in small batches. They're good for sipping—perhaps with a splash of tonic and lime—but don't waste these rums in a cocktail!

SPICED (OR FLAVORED) RUMS: A new trend, these rums can be white, golden, or dark. They are infused with additives such as spices, vanilla, or citrus, and they add extra flavor to blended drinks.

151 PROOF RUMS: Also known as overproof rums, these are very potent—and flammable. They are rough tasting and should not be drunk straight; rather, they are used in tiny amounts to boost the alcohol content of a drink—they're often floated on top of a drink and sometimes ignited. Because of its high alcohol content, overproof rum is not available in all countries. Dark rum can be substituted when a drink recipe calls for 151 proof rum.

Rum Tasting

While islanders have been sipping their aged rums neat for generations, rum has only recently gained a reputation as a sipping drink in the United States, where it is well on its way to being the next designer drink, following in the footsteps of scotch, vodka, and tequila. Some aged rums on the market are on a par with an excellent cognac or port and are exquisite taken neat or sipped on the rocks (perhaps with a squeeze of lime). A few favorite sipping rums include

MATUSALEM RUM

PLANTATION OLD RESERVE RUM from Barbados (there are Plantation Old Reserve Rums from the islands of Jamaica and Trinidad as well)

BARBENCOURT

APPLETON ESTATE EXTRA from Jamaica

BOTRAN AÑEJO from Guatemala

BACARDI OCHOS AÑOS

EL DORADO SPECIAL RESERVE

MOUNT GAY EXTRA GOLD

PAMPERO ANIVERSARIO from Venezuela

FLOR DE CAÑA GRAND RESERVE from Nicaragua

GOSLING'S BLACK SEAL from Bermuda

COCKSPUR V.S.O.R. from Barbados

Helpful Conversions

$^1/_4$ ounce = $1^1/_2$ teaspoons
$^1/_2$ ounce = 1 tablespoon
$^3/_4$ ounce = 1 tablespoon plus 2 teaspoons
$1^1/_2$ ounces = 3 tablespoons
8 ounces = 1 cup

Cocktails

There's naught, no doubt, so much
the spirit calms as rum and true religion.
–Lord Byron

A colorful trio of pink, white, and green, this and the next two frozen cocktails (pages 20–22) are creamy, bright, and not too sweet, and they have a delectable taste and body. Served together, their colors are gorgeous—make a batch of all three and you have a party. Each recipe makes two large drinks of 9 ounces each or four small drinks that fit into 5-ounce glasses (or one huge drink in an enormous tiki drink bowl).

Seafoam

This minty-green drink is more tart than sweet and quite refreshing. Adding a bit of half-and-half diminishes the wateriness that you often find in frozen drinks. (The addition of cream is a bartender's secret to give frozen drinks a bit of body and make them smooth.) Garnish with fresh flowers and serve with aloha.

> *2 ounces Demerara rum*
> *1 1/2 ounces sour mix (page 23)*
> *1 ounce blue curaçao*
> *1 ounce Midori*
> *1 ounce freshly squeezed lemon juice*
> *1/4 ounce half-and-half*
> *2 1/2 cups ice cubes*

Combine all the ingredients in a blender and blend until smooth, about 10 seconds. Pulse a few times if the ice sticks in the blades. Serve immediately.

Serves 2

Alo means "experience," and *ha* means "breath of life." So when you say "aloha," you invite people to experience a breath of life with you.

Mary Ann and Ginger

In a nod to *Gilligan's Island*, this drink has a silky tropical fruit flavor with a subtle ginger finish that rings at the back of your mouth. There's not much alcohol in this drink, which is good since you'll want to drink plenty. The bubblegum pink color looks great in a martini glass. The half-and-half gives it body (as if Ginger needed it). Garnish with fresh flowers.

1 ounce ginger cordial (see note)

4 ounces guava purée (see note)

2 ounces white rum

2 ounces cranberry juice

1 ounce pineapple juice

1 ounce grenadine

$^1/_4$ ounce half-and-half

2 $^1/_2$ cups ice cubes

Combine all the ingredients in a blender and blend until smooth, about 10 seconds. Pulse a few times if the ice sticks in the blades. Serve immediately.

Serves 2

NOTES:

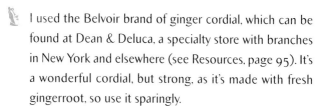

I used the Belvoir brand of ginger cordial, which can be found at Dean & Deluca, a specialty store with branches in New York and elsewhere (see Resources, page 95). It's a wonderful cordial, but strong, as it's made with fresh gingerroot, so use it sparingly.

Guava purée is simply puréed guava (skinned and pitted) with sugar. It has no carbonation. If you can't find it in a store (it's usually available in Latino markets), simply purée fresh guava and add enough sugar until it is sweet to your liking.

Tiki drinks and food can be served in many settings—even a feminine luncheon. You don't need to run down to the party store and stock up on tiki torches and plastic leis—all you need are good food, people, and fresh flowers for a party. Surprise your guests by serving tiki-style cuisine with Granny's silver, china, and linen napkins.

Shark's Tooth

Not too sweet, this bright drink tastes of oranges and sour mix, with a coconut finish and a delicate coconut perfume from the coconut syrup. A milky color, this drink is pretty garnished with pink flowers.

> 2 $^1/_2$ ounces golden rum
>
> 1 $^1/_2$ ounces pineapple juice
>
> 1 $^1/_2$ ounces sour mix (page 23)
>
> 1 ounce coconut syrup (see note)
>
> 3 ounces unsweetened coconut milk (see note)
>
> Juice of $^1/_2$ lime
>
> $^1/_2$ ounce Cointreau
>
> 2 $^1/_2$ cups ice cubes

Combine all the ingredients in a blender and blend until smooth, about 10 seconds. Pulse a few times if the ice sticks in the blades. Serve immediately.

Serves 2

NOTES:

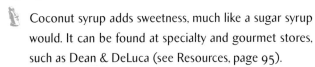 Coconut syrup adds sweetness, much like a sugar syrup would. It can be found at specialty and gourmet stores, such as Dean & DeLuca (see Resources, page 95).

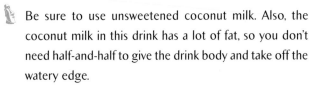 Be sure to use unsweetened coconut milk. Also, the coconut milk in this drink has a lot of fat, so you don't need half-and-half to give the drink body and take off the watery edge.

SOUR MIX

To make a delicious sour mix, combine 1 part frozen lemonade concentrate with 2 parts frozen limeade concentrate and mix with half the amount of water indicated on the cans. If you have leftover frozen lemonade concentrate, mix it with club soda and garnish with lime and lemon slices for an inspired lemonade.

· Good flowers and plants for
garnishing a tiki drink:
orchids, gardenias, bougainvillea, mint

· Pretty flowers for making leis:
orchids, daisies, carnations, cornflowers,
mums, asters, dahlias

Great White

This drink is Pacific-inspired, with a hint of Tahitian vanilla and coconut milk. Think surf, sharks, whales...

> 1 ¹/₂ ounces spiced rum
> ³/₄ ounce Tahitian vanilla syrup (see note)
> 3 ounces unsweetened coconut milk
> Pinch of freshly grated nutmeg for garnish

Pour the rum, syrup, and coconut milk over ice in a rocks glass. Cover with a cocktail shaker, shake to blend, and garnish with the nutmeg.

Serves 1

NOTE: Use the kind of vanilla syrup that is used in coffees and sodas and is sold at Italian shops or coffee stores.

For 300 years, British sailors each received a daily two-ounce ration of rum for good health.

Red Skies at Night...Sailor's Delight

Inspired by the idea of a French-style Polynesian cocktail, this is a clean, light aperitif that makes a perfect predinner drink. The cassis differs in weight from the cranberry juice and creates an eerie sunset effect as the darker color settles at the bottom. This drink is refreshing on a hot summer night.

  2 ounces white rum
  2 ounces cranberry juice
  1 ounce cassis
  1 ounce sour mix (page 23)
  Club soda
  ¹/₂ lemon

Add ice to a highball glass, pour over the first 4 ingredients, and top off with club soda. Squeeze the lemon half into the drink, then drop in the rind, and stir to blend.

Serves 1

Walk the Plank

This is a velvety after-dinner drink. As a variation, you can add milk to taste–on a cold night, warm milk. It's meant to be sipped or tossed back from a shot glass. Once you've experienced it you will definitely feel like you have walked into the deep end...

$1/2$ ounce dark rum
$1/2$ ounce spiced rum
$1/2$ ounce Frangelico
$1/2$ ounce Kahlúa

Measure ingredients straight from the bottles into a 2-ounce shot glass.

Serves 1

After Midnight

Make this tasty drink quickly; if you tarry and allow the ingredients to relax in the ice, the drink will become watery and change its taste.

> 1 ¹/₂ ounces dark rum
> 1 ounce Kahlúa
> 1 ¹/₂ ounces piña colada mix

Fill a metal cocktail shaker with ice and the drink ingredients. Shake until a frost appears on the shaker (about 15 seconds), strain into a cocktail glass, and serve.

Serves 1

A tropical drink always tastes better on a white sandy beach in a palm-fringed lagoon than it does in, say, the Tonga Room at San Francisco's Fairmont Hotel. But if you can't get to the beach, light the tiki torches in your backyard, close your eyes, put on some Jimmy Vaughan, whip up some tiki drinks, and dream.

Painkiller

This adaptation of the famous British Virgin Islands drink is unusual in that, while the fruity coconut flavor punches forward, it's not cloyingly sweet. Rather, the coconut provides just a touch of sweetness, while the dusting of nutmeg gives the drink a pleasing spiciness. For this drink you can use a rocks glass or a fancy tiki glass.

> *2 ounces pineapple juice*
> *1 1/4 ounces golden rum*
> *1/2 ounce freshly squeezed orange juice*
> *1/2 ounce coconut syrup (see page 22)*
> *Pinch of freshly grated nutmeg for garnish*

Fill the glass with ice and add the first 4 ingredients. Cover with a cocktail shaker, shake to blend, and garnish with the nutmeg.

Serves 1

Tropical Moment

This pretty lime-green drink is perfect in a luau setting. It has a nice tropical fruity flavor from the peach and pineapple, but it's not overly sweet.

> 1 1/2 *ounces white rum*
> 1/2 *ounce peach schnapps*
> 1 *ounce Midori*
> 1 *ounce pineapple juice*
> 1 *ounce sour mix (page 23)*
> 1/4 *lime for garnish*

Fill a rocks or highball glass with ice and pour all ingredients over the ice. Cover with a cocktail shaker, shake to blend, and garnish with the 1/4 lime.

Serves 1

The first rum sour was made in Barbados and served in a conch shell.

Tall Blue Drink

This tropical blue coconut drink is all about the beach—
suntan lotion, waves, being on holiday. It's gorgeous garnished with a fresh pink tropical flower.

>   1 ½ ounces white rum
>   1 ounce coconut syrup (see page 22)
>   1 ounce blue curaçao
>   1 ounce pineapple juice
>   3 ounces sour mix (page 23)
>   Club soda
>   Lime wedge for garnish

Add ice to a highball glass and pour over the first 5 ingredients (rum through sour mix). Top off with club soda, stir to
blend, squeeze the lime into the drink, and drop in the
squeezed wedge.

Serves 1

Hibiscus

The hibiscus flower was the color inspiration for this pink drink. Not particularly sour or sweet, this is a clean cocktail with a broad flavor palette, made possible by the Lillet, which bartenders use to open up the flavors of a drink.

> *2 ounces golden rum*
> *1 ounce Lillet white*
> *1 ounce guava purée (see page 21)*
> *1 ounce freshly squeezed lemon juice*
> *¹/₄ ounce grenadine*

Fill a metal cocktail shaker with ice and the drink ingredients. Shake until a frost appears on the shaker (about 15 seconds) and strain into an attractive martini glass. Garnish with a fresh tropical flower, if you like.

Serves 1

Coco-Nut

This elegant cocktail is a late-night sort of drink. With its restrained, toasted coffee-like flavor, it's good after dinner or at 4 A.M. Be sure to use a high-quality Kahlúa. This drink is pretty in a martini glass, garnished with a white flower. As a variation, you might wet and dust the rim of the glass with powdered chocolate.

1 ½ ounces spiced rum
1 ounce Kahlúa
1 ounce dry vermouth

Fill a metal cocktail shaker with ice and the drink ingredients. Shake until a frost appears on the shaker (about 15 seconds), strain into a martini glass, and serve.

Serves 1

Kon-Tiki

This drink is for the guy whose wife cons him into going to a tiki bar—in other words, the nontiki drinker's tiki drink. Demerara rum has an exquisite woodiness (it's great as a sipping rum, too), which is highlighted by the drink's subtle coconut flavor. This is a cocktail that a whiskey drinker would like.

1 ½ ounces Demerara rum
1 ounce coconut syrup (see page 22)
Club soda
Lime wedge

Fill a rocks glass with ice and add the rum and coconut syrup. Top off with club soda, squeeze the lime into the drink, and stir. Drop in the lime wedge and a decorative stir stick.

Serves 1

Nancy's Grass Skirt

This light green drink is a bit sour, with an exotic aftertaste of lemongrass. Easy to make, it's a bartender's favorite (and one of mine, too!).

> 1 ¹/₂ ounces white rum
> 1 ¹/₂ ounces Belvoir lime and lemongrass cordial (see note)
> 1 ounce sour mix (page 23)
> ¹/₂ lime
> Thai basil or mint for garnish

Fill a rocks glass with ice and add the first 3 ingredients. Squeeze the lime half into the drink and drop in the rind. Cover with a cocktail shaker, shake, and garnish with a sprig of Thai basil or mint.

Serves 1

NOTE: Belvoir lime and lemongrass cordial is a fruit cordial made with fresh lime and lemongrass extract (available at Dean & DeLuca; see Resources, page 95). It's worth mail-ordering it simply to be able to make this drink!

Tahitian Sunset

With plenty of juice, this pretty, not-too-sweet pastel drink is
an ideal fruity summertime beverage for people who don't
want to drink too much alcohol. As this drink sits, it will separate, and the darker colors will gravitate to the bottom, sort
of like a sunset. Go all out with the paper parasols, plastic
monkeys, and fruit garnishes on this one.

1 ¹/₂ ounces Demerara rum
4 ounces pineapple juice
1 ounce freshly squeezed orange juice
1 ¹/₂ teaspoons grenadine
1 teaspoon almond syrup
Pineapple or orange slice, or maraschino cherry for garnish

Fill a highball glass with ice. Pour the first 5 ingredients into
the glass, cover with a cocktail shaker, shake to blend, and garnish with the fruit.

Serves 1

NOTE: Almond syrup (also called orgeat syrup) can be found
in large liquor stores, specialty stores, and coffee shops (see
Resources, page 95).

What could be more iconic of
a tiki drink than a colorful
paper parasol? Don the
Beachcomber borrowed
the idea from Chinese
restaurants in the United
States and started using
them in the 1930s. To
shield the ice cubes from
the sun and rain? Nope. Just
to make the drinks fetching.

Hawaii Five-O

Inspired by the island of Kauai, this is a new drink in the tiki tradition. While this recipe serves one, it could easily be scaled up and served as a fruity fresh punch.

Juice of 1/2 lemon
Juice of 1/2 lime
Juice of 1/2 orange
1 1/2 ounces golden rum
2 ounces mango drink (see note)
Sliced fruit for garnish

Fill a rocks glass with ice. Pour the lemon, lime, and orange juices over the ice, add rum, and top with mango drink. Cover with a cocktail shaker, shake to blend, and garnish with fruit wheels or wedges.

Serves 1

NOTE: You can find mango drink at Indian or Latino grocery stores or online at Sadaf.com. Just make sure that you use mango drink, not a carbonated mango blend or a mango purée.

Cocktail shakers date back to 7000 B.C. in South America. They became the rage in the United States after the repeal of Prohibition in 1933, finding their way into many Hollywood movies of that era as symbols of stylish elegance. The popularity of cocktail shakers is still strong; they have been manufactured in many whimsical shapes, from the Boston lighthouse to airplanes to barbells.

Mahukona

Adapted from a drink of the same name created by Trader Vic, this smooth, well-balanced cocktail is terrific on a hot evening. The brown sugar brings out the sweetness of the woody rum and helps soften and smooth over the tartness of the lemon, making the lemon a cleanser, rather than a sharp ingredient. If you like whiskey sours, you'll love this fresh-tasting drink.

1 teaspoon light brown sugar
1 ounce hot water
1 ounce pineapple juice
1 ounce golden rum
1/2 ounce triple sec
1/2 ounce freshly squeezed lemon juice
2 dashes Angostura bitters

Dilute the brown sugar in the hot water. Fill a rocks glass with ice and add all the ingredients. Cover with a cocktail shaker, shake, and serve.

Serves 1

No man can be stiff with something on his head.
—Trader Vic, referring to the custom of men wearing head leis at a luau

A Passionate Kiss

This tropical drink is from Duffy's Love Shack, which Tim and Liz Duffy started in an alleyway in St. Thomas in 1995. Later that year, the bar became the unwitting home of a forty-foot sailboat as Hurricane Marilyn barrelled across the island, and Duffy's was rebuilt in Red Hook, where it's been dubbed the coolest parking lot bar in the Caribbean.

> 1 $^1/_2$ ounces golden rum
> 1 ounce Passoa passionfruit liqueur (see note)
> 1 $^1/_2$ ounces passionfruit juice (see note)
> $^1/_4$ ounce freshly squeezed lime juice
> $^3/_4$ ounce cane syrup (see note)
> 1 ounce strawberry purée (see note)

Combine all the ingredients in a blender and blend until smooth. Serve over ice in a highball glass or your favorite tiki mug.

Serves 1

NOTE: Passoa passionfruit liqueur is available at most liquor stores. Passionfruit juice, cane syrup, and strawberry purée are available in Caribbean markets. You can also make strawberry purée by combining fresh strawberries with a little lemon juice and water in a blender.

Short Hoist

Trader Vic called his shot drinks "short hoists," which I think is marvelous, and which applies to this eminently shootable drink. The color of Windex, this pretty blue drink has a nice sweet-sour pull to it. Shots are very popular at Nancy's bar at Eleven; people order a round and toast someone. Serve a round of these to friends on a tray at a party and toast someone's good fortune.

> 1 $^1/_2$ ounces white rum
> 1 ounce blue curaçao
> 1 ounce sour mix (page 23)
> Juice of $^1/_2$ lime

Fill a metal cocktail shaker with ice and the drink ingredients. Shake until a frost appears on the shaker (about 15 seconds), strain into shot glasses, and serve.

Serves 2

Before capturing Fort Ticonderoga in 1775, Ethan Allen stopped by for a pop of rum at the Catamount Tavern in Vermont.

Mai Tai

Wanting a new rum drink, Victor (Trader Vic) Bergeron mixed his first Mai Tai in 1944 for some visiting Tahitian friends, who proclaimed it *"mai tai–roe ae"* (which means "out of this world–the best"). This version is from Franklin Eck, a connoisseur of Mai Tais and perhaps the original Trader Vic's fan. He spent a lot of time in the South Pacific in the 1950s and is known by name at Trader Vic's restaurants all over the world. (His favorite Trader Vic's? The one at the Beverly Hilton, which is also Nancy Sinatra's favorite hangout.)

> 1 1/2 ounces Mai Tai Mix (opposite page)
> 2 ounces freshly squeezed lime juice, 1/4 spent lime
>   reserved
> 2 ounces dark rum
> 1 ounce golden rum
> Dash of Angostura bitters
> Sprig of mint for garnish
> Maraschino cherry for garnish
> Pineapple wedge for garnish

Fill a double old-fashioned glass with crushed ice and add liquid ingredients. Cover with a cocktail shaker and shake to blend. Garnish with the sprig of mint, the cherry, the pineapple wedge, and the reserved 1/4 lime.

Serves 1

Anyone who says I didn't create
[the Mai Tai] is a dirty stinker.
—Victor Bergeron

MAI TAI MIX

1 ounce orange curaçao

¹/₂ ounce orgeat syrup

Orgeat syrup is an almond syrup that can be found in large liquor stores, specialty stores, and coffee shops (see Resources, page 95).

Passion Fizz

This light, refreshing drink is a bit of tropical paradise. It reminds me of eating ripened mangos in a bathing suit while standing knee-deep in azure water.

1 ¹/₂ ounces golden rum
1 ounce passionfruit syrup (see page 56)
Club soda
Sprig of spearmint for garnish
Lime wedge for garnish

Fill a rocks glass with crushed ice. Add the rum and syrup, and top off with club soda. Stir, then garnish with the spearmint and lime wedge.

Serves 1

After Admiral Nelson died aboard ship during the Battle of Trafalgar, his body was preserved for burial in a cask of his favorite rum.

Hurricane

The Hurricane was developed at Pat O'Brien's restaurant in New Orleans in the 1960s and is now a classic New Orleans drink, popular at Mardi Gras. Though Pat O'Brien's isn't even a wee bit Polynesian, the Hurricane has been imitated at tiki bars everywhere.

> 1 ounce dark rum
> 1 1/2 ounces white rum
> 1 1/2 ounces passionfruit syrup (see page 56)
> 1/2 ounce freshly squeezed lime juice
> 2 teaspoons superfine sugar
> Splash of grenadine
> Lime or orange wedge for garnish

Fill a highball glass with ice. Pour all ingredients except fruit wedge into the glass, cover with a cocktail shaker, and shake to blend. Garnish with a lime or orange wedge and serve immediately.

Serves 1

Blue Hawaiian

The original Blue Hawaiian was developed by Harry K. Yee, a legendary Honolulu bartender who knew what tourists wanted. It's still one of the most requested drinks in Hawaii, with the blue curaçao evoking the waters off the islands of Hawaii. In this version, the coconut gives the drink a soft mellow milkiness that's delicious. Serve with aloha.

> *3 ounces pineapple juice*
> *¹/₂ ounce blue curaçao*
> *1 ounce golden rum*
> *1 ounce cream of coconut*
> *Lime wedge for garnish*

Fill a highball glass with ice and pour the first 4 ingredients into the glass. Cover with a cocktail shaker, shake to blend, and drop in the lime wedge. Serve immediately.

Serves 1

While decorating a tropical drink with a fresh flower seems as natural as using an olive in a martini or a maraschino cherry in a Shirley Temple, it's a relatively recent invention. Harry K. Yee, who was the head bartender at the Hilton Hawaiian Village for over thirty years and created many famous drinks, including the Blue Hawaiian, Wahine's Delight, Tropical Itch, and Hawaiian Eye, is quoted as saying: "We used to use a sugarcane stick, and people would chew on the stick, then put it in the ashtray. When the ashes and cane stuck together it made a real mess, so I put the orchids in the drinks to make the ashtrays easier to clean. I wasn't thinking about romance; I was being practical."

Zombie

This legendary drink was created by Hollywood barmeister Donn Beach. Though he never gave away his recipe, here's a tasty approximation. Adding the grenadine gives this drink a pretty sunrise effect.

> 1 ¹/₂ ounces golden rum
> 1 ounce dark rum
> 1 ¹/₂ ounces pineapple juice
> 1 ¹/₂ ounces pink grapefruit juice
> 2 teaspoons superfine sugar
> 1 tablespoon lime juice
> ¹/₂ teaspoon grenadine
> 3 teaspoons passionfruit syrup (see page 56)
> 1 teaspoon 151 proof rum
> Fruit wedge for garnish
> Fresh mint for garnish
> Maraschino cherry for garnish

Fill a metal cocktail shaker with ice and the drink ingredients. Shake until a frost appears on the shaker (about 15 seconds), and strain. Garnish with the fruit wedge, mint, and cherry.

OPTIONAL: Instead of mixing the 151 proof rum into the drink, float it on top of the finished drink and lightly sprinkle with confectioners' sugar.

Serves 1

At the 1939 World's Fair in Flushing, New York, the supertechnologized "world of tomorrow" stood before thousands of patrons. It was a runway full of newfangled washing machines, kitchenware, aerodynamic sculptures, and weapons galore. But anyone looking for a high-tech escape from streamlined excess had only to take refuge in the Hurricane Bar, where a new cocktail was introduced to the world: the Zombie.

–Joseph Lanza in *The Cocktail: The Influence of Spirits on the American Psyche*

Missionary's Downfall

In this drink, the lime's tartness is balanced by the sweetness of pineapple and a hint of mint. I love the name of this drink (which was dreamed up by Donn Beach)—it's so much more refined than the in-your-face drink names of the 1970s, such as Screaming Orgasm.

> *Sprig of mint, leaves only*
> *1/3 cup fresh pineapple chunks*
> *1/2 ounce apricot liqueur*
> *1/2 ounce caramel syrup or sugar syrup (see note)*
> *1 ounce light rum*
> *1 1/2 ounces freshly squeezed lime juice*
> *4 ounces ice*

Combine all the ingredients in a blender and blend until smooth, about 10 seconds. Pulse a few times if the ice sticks in the blades. Serve immediately.

Serves 1

NOTE: Sugar syrup is also called rock candy syrup or simple syrup. To make your own, boil 3 parts of granulated sugar in 1 part of water until it dissolves (about 5 minutes).

Singapore Sling

This drink was invented at the Raffles Hotel in Singapore in the early 1900s. The name may derive from the German word *schlingen*, which means "to swallow." The vanilla rounds out the drink's fruity cherry flavor, both enhancing the botanicals of the gin and giving the drink a bit more complexity. You can also omit the traditional cherry brandy and call it a Singapore Slung.

> *2 ounces premium gin*
> *1 ounce grenadine*
> *1 teaspoon superfine sugar*
> *1 teaspoon vanilla syrup (see page 24)*
> *Juice of ¹/₂ lemon*
> *1 teaspoon cherry brandy*
> *Club soda*

Fill a highball glass with ice. Pour the first 6 ingredients into the glass, cover with a cocktail shaker, and shake to blend. Top off with club soda and serve immediately.

Serves 1

Tropical Itch

When Honolulu bartender Harry K. Yee served the Tropical Itch with a Chinese back-scratcher in 1957, he not only made his drink famous, but also created a high demand for back-scratchers. This adaptation is a simple rum drink for a tropical night.

1 ¹/₂ ounces pineapple juice
¹/₂ ounce passionfruit syrup (see note)
2 ounces dark rum
Juice of ¹/₂ lemon

Fill a highball glass with ice. Pour all ingredients into the glass, stir, and serve.

Serves 1

NOTE: Many liquor stores carry passionfruit syrup, or you can mail-order it (see Resources, page 95). Passionfruit syrup is also delicious drizzled over ice cream or combined with club soda for a refreshing drink; or mix it with a little hot sauce and butter, brush it on fresh quartered pineapple, and grill.

Blue Lagoon

While a Blue Lagoon is traditionally made with vodka, using tequila adds a new twist to a classic Polynesian cocktail. This drink is dedicated to my friend Jeff Kleiser, who finally inherited his parents' dented cocktail shaker. It's important that you have all the ingredients at your fingertips when you begin to mix this drink so that it doesn't get watery as the ice melts.

>   *2 ounces premium tequila*
>   *1 ounce Grand Marnier*
>   *$^1/_2$ ounce blue curaçao*
>   *$^1/_2$ ounce sour mix (page 23)*
>   *Juice of 1 lime*
>   *Lime wedges for garnish*

Fill a metal cocktail shaker with ice and the drink ingredients. Give two quick shakes and strain into martini-style glasses. Garnish with the lime wedges and serve.

Serves 2

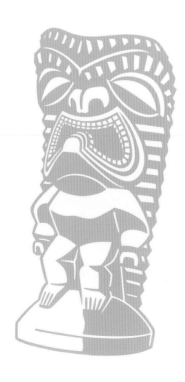

Paradise Overdose

This rum punch recipe was given to novelist Brian Antoni by his grandfather, who was buried in a cask of rum, as specified by his will; he didn't want to face the afterlife without his favorite spirit. Brian named his first novel, *Paradise Overdose,* after this drink. The recipe is based on this old Caribbean slave jingle: "one of sour, two of sweet, three of strong, four of weak, and a little bitter for good luck." You can substitute 1 ounce of sour mix (page 23) for the lime juice and passionfruit juice.

one of sour

> $^1/_2$ ounce freshly squeezed lime juice and $^1/_2$ ounce passion-fruit juice (see page 41)

two of sweet

>   1 ounce sugar syrup (page 52)
>   1 ounce grenadine

three of strong

>   2 ounces dark rum
>   1 ounce coconut or spiced rum

four of weak

>   4 ice cubes with Maraschino cherries frozen in the centers
>   A few dashes of Angostura bitters
>   Lime wedge or orange slice for garnish

Pour all the ingredients into a highball glass filled with ice, and stir. Garnish with the lime wedge or slice of orange.

Serves 1

The early colonists in America drank 12 million gallons of rum per year—almost 4 gallons per person.

Suffering Bastard

This nineteenth-century gem was named at Shepheard's Hotel in Cairo when a few Brits at the bar christened their drinks as such after misunderstanding the bartender's comment about his "poor, suffering bar steward." Slightly astringent and almost bubbly, this drink is refreshing on a hot day. The lack of rum sets it apart from many tiki drinks.

1 1/2 ounces gin
1/2 ounce bourbon
3 ounces ginger ale
Juice of 1/2 lime
Sprig of mint for garnish

Pour the drink ingredients into an ice-filled glass. Cover with a cocktail shaker, shake briefly to blend, and garnish with the mint.

Serves 1

Appetizers

*Oh to be born on one of the South Sea Isles
as a so-called savage, for once to enjoy
human existence as pure and untainted by
a fake aftertaste.*
—Johann Wolfgang von Goethe

Chicken Satay

Inspired by Singaporean street food, this Southeast Asian–style satay (or "meat on a stick," as Trader Vic called satays) is quick and easy to prepare. All you need to do is marinate, skewer, and grill. Short skewers are easier to work with and make a pretty appetizer. If you use bamboo or wooden skewers, soak them for at least 20 minutes before cooking. Serve with the Spicy Peanut Dipping Sauce (page 88) or simply with a bit of sour cream combined with chopped cucumbers, lemon juice, and chopped fresh mint.

1 pound boneless, skinless chicken breasts

MARINADE

1 teaspoon ground coriander

$1/2$ teaspoon turmeric

1 clove garlic, finely chopped

1 tablespoon sugar

1 teaspoon tamarind paste (see note)

$1/4$ cup unsweetened coconut milk

Juice of $1/2$ lime

Butter lettuce leaves

Cilantro sprigs for garnish

Lime wedges for garnish

Cut the chicken into $1/4$-inch slices that run the length of the chicken breast. If you find it difficult to trim so thin, put the chicken into the freezer for 20 minutes for easier cutting.

Place the chicken strips in a large bowl. Add all the marinade ingredients and toss until the chicken is well coated. Cover and refrigerate for a minimum of 2 hours and up to 24 hours.

When you are ready to cook the satay, prepare the grill. Thread each chicken slice onto a skewer, working each skewer in and out of the meat. Cook over medium-high heat for $3 1/2$ minutes per side, or until the juice runs clear. (You can also cook under the broiler for 3 to 4 minutes on each side.)

Serve on a bed of crisp butter lettuce leaves and garnish with the cilantro sprigs and lime wedges.

Serves 4 as an entrée, 6 as an appetizer

NOTE: Tamarind paste is a tart, fruity flavored paste found in ethnic grocery stores.

Thai Curry Spring Rolls

These spring rolls have a subtle, back-of-the-mouth heat that's a good contrast to a cool, sweet drink. This dish is pretty served on a bed of butter lettuce and delicious served with a thin salty dipping sauce, such as ponzu sauce, which is made with sesame oil, soy sauce, chiles, and garlic (available at Asian and specialty food stores; see Resources, page 95). You could also serve them with Spicy Mango-Apricot Sauce (page 89).

6 ounces pork butt, coarsely chopped
1/2 inch fresh ginger, peeled and sliced
1 clove garlic
12 sprigs cilantro
1 teaspoon ground kaffir lime leaves (see note)
1 teaspoon Thai green curry paste
2 eggs
1 teaspoon water
Spring roll wrappers (see note)
Canola oil

Place the first 6 ingredients (pork through curry paste) in a food processor and pulse until ingredients have a coarsely ground consistency.

Whisk the eggs together in a bowl with the teaspoon of water to make an egg wash. On your work surface, lay out 4 wrappers diagonally (with corners pointing toward you) and brush egg wash on the entire perimeter of each wrapper. Put 1/4 of the pork mixture in the center of each wrapper, molding it into a long cigar shape from the left point to the right point of the square. Fold the bottom over the mixture, then the left and right sides, and then roll it up.

Line a plate with paper towels to drain the spring rolls, and set it beside the stove. Heat ¹/₂-inch oil in a 12-inch frying pan over medium-high heat until it reaches 350°. If the oil is smoking, it's too hot. Gently place the spring rolls in the oil and cook, turning to brown all sides, until golden brown, about 6 or 7 minutes. Remove the rolls and drain them on the paper towel–lined plate. Serve hot. (If you are cooking more than 4 spring rolls, put the cooked rolls in a 250° oven to keep them warm.)

Makes 4 spring rolls

NOTES:

- The rich taste of kaffir lime leaves mixes well with other ingredients, for a distinctive, refreshing taste that is uniquely Thai. (See Resources, page 95.)
- Spring roll wrappers can be found in the refrigerated fresh produce section of most good supermarkets.

Tamarind-Glazed Beef

With its sweet and sour glaze, this Hawaiian-inspired dish is good food for a luau or an outdoor barbecue. If you cut the sirloin into thin strips and skewer it, it's a pretty hors d'oeuvre; cut into larger portions, it can be served as an entrée for lunch or dinner. If you're using wood or bamboo skewers, soak them for 20 minutes before you use them.

1 pound sirloin tips

1 shallot, finely chopped

2 tablespoons tamarind paste (see page 65)

$1/4$ cup dark rum

2 tablespoons soy sauce

$1/4$ cup dark brown sugar

1 canned chipotle pepper (in adobo sauce), finely chopped

1 teaspoon adobo sauce

1 teaspoon sesame oil

Salt

Freshly ground pepper

$1/4$ cup white sesame seeds for garnish

Slice the sirloin against the grain into 16 thin strips if you are serving as an hors d'oeuvre, or cut into 4 four-ounce portions if an entrée.

To make the marinade, combine the shallot, tamarind paste, rum, soy sauce, brown sugar, chipotle pepper, adobo sauce, and sesame oil in a medium bowl. Whisk ingredients together to blend in the brown sugar. Add salt and pepper to taste. Add the beef to the marinade and marinate, refrigerated, for 2 to 6 hours.

Prepare the grill. If serving as an hors d'oeuvre, thread the strips onto skewers. Cook the meat on the grill over high heat, 3 minutes on each side for skewers or 5 to 6 minutes on each side for 4-ounce portions.

Garnish with a sprinkling of sesame seeds.

Serves 4 as an entrée, 8 as an appetizer

NOTE: If you don't have time to grill, you can broil the skewers for 3 to 4 minutes on each side.

People are sometimes intimidated by the idea of a luau, but basically, it's an outdoor barbecue with tropical touches thrown in. Long the symbol of Hawaiian hospitality, luaus always include good food, music, and flowers. You can keep your luau simple, or you can turn it into a big party. Traditionally luaus were a way of giving thanks to the gods for having survived an ocean passage, but today luaus celebrate birthdays, anniversaries—even moving into a new home. People often wear aloha shirts or long dresses, and it's customary in the islands for the host to greet each woman with a kiss, a lei, and flowers for her hair, while the hostess greets the men with kisses and head leis. There are flowers everywhere—on the buffet table, at the bar, on the people. The luau traditionally begins with a prayer, and there's plenty of hula dancing, singing, eating, and music provided by ukulele, guitar, steel guitar, and bass. The most famous luau was given by King Kamehameha III in 1843, with 10,000 guests enjoying 271 hogs, 3 whole oxen, 1,820 fresh fish, and various delicacies.

Maui Gazpacho

Pineapple adds a sweet Hawaiian touch to this refreshing soup and balances out the tartness of the tomatillos. For a stylish dish, ladle the diced vegetables into a mound in each bowl and pour the tomato mixture around them.

2 red bell peppers, seeded and stems removed

2 green bell peppers, seeded and stems removed

2 yellow bell peppers, seeded and stems removed

2 cucumbers, peeled

1 red onion

1 cup pineapple chunks

6 fresh tomatillos, husks removed

1 avocado, peeled and pitted

$1/4$ cup packed cilantro leaves and stems

$1/4$ cup cider vinegar

4 cups tomato juice or tomato and vegetable juice blend

2 tablespoons extra virgin olive oil

3 dashes hot sauce

1 green onion, white and green parts, chopped

Salt

Freshly ground pepper

2 tablespoons toasted coconut for garnish (see note)

Finely chop the first 9 ingredients (red bell peppers through cilantro) and combine in a large bowl. Season to taste with salt and pepper. In a separate bowl, combine the liquids and the chopped green onions. Season to taste with salt and pepper.

To serve, place a cup of the vegetable mixture in the centers of each of 8 shallow bowls, pour the tomato juice mixture around the vegetables, and garnish with toasted coconut.

Serves 8

NOTE: To make the toasted coconut, preheat the oven to 400°. Put packaged shredded coconut on a baking sheet in the oven for 4 to 5 minutes, or until the coconut has golden-brown edges.

Macadamia Soba Noodles

This savory noodle dish can be served either hot or cold. If you find it's not salty enough for your taste, add up to a tablespoon more of soy sauce.

1 pound soba noodles

3 ounces macadamia nuts

$1/4$ cup plus 2 tablespoons sesame oil

2 cloves garlic, finely chopped

$1/2$ inch fresh ginger, peeled and finely chopped

2 tablespoons soy sauce

2 tablespoons rice wine vinegar

2 green onions, white and half the green parts

$1/2$ cup cilantro leaves

Cook the noodles in rapidly boiling water for 7 or 8 minutes, until al dente. Drain and set aside in a large bowl.

Preheat oven to 350°. Place the macadamia nuts on a baking sheet and toast in the oven for 6 minutes. Remove and set aside to cool, at least 10 minutes.

To make the sauce, heat 2 tablespoons of the sesame oil over medium heat in a 9-inch sauté pan. Sauté the garlic and ginger for 90 seconds. Remove the pan from the burner and add the remaining sesame oil, soy sauce, and rice wine vinegar. Whisk to incorporate the ingredients and set aside.

Coarsely chop the cooled macadamia nuts, green onions, and cilantro and add to the cooked soba noodles. Pour the sauce over the noodles and stir to blend all the ingredients.

Serves 4 as an entrée, 6 as an appetizer

Lemon and Watercress Tea Sandwiches

This and the next two sandwich recipes are perfect for a luncheon or a quick and easy afternoon cocktail party. Serve with the colorful frozen cocktails on pages 19 to 22. The drinks and sandwiches can all be made in an hour or so. Or these sandwiches can be served as hors d'oeuvres. As an alternative, try adding poached shrimp, sliced in half lengthwise, to the sandwiches. Or, if you have leftover chicken satay, simply place the chicken strips on top of the watercress and blended sour cream, roll them up in the bread slices, and serve whole as sandwiches or slice into hors d'oeuvres.

1/2 cup sour cream
Zest of 1 lemon
1/2 teaspoon salt
1/2 teaspoon freshly ground black pepper
12 very thin slices white bread, crusts removed
1 bunch watercress, stems removed

In a bowl, blend the sour cream, lemon zest, salt, and pepper. Spread onto 6 slices of bread. Place watercress on top and top with the remaining bread slices. Cut each sandwich into 4 triangles and serve.

Makes 24 sandwiches

Cucumber and Smoked Salmon Cocktail Sandwiches

This easy fusion sandwich marries English cucumber to Nordic smoked salmon and Japanese wasabi. The wasabi is just enough to add flavor, not heat (after all, one doesn't want to cry when eating with friends). Buy the best smoked salmon you can afford. You can turn this sandwich into an elegant cold hors d'oeuvre by serving it as an open-faced sandwich with wasabi roe (beautiful bright green roe made with wasabi, available in the fish department of many supermarkets). Quarter the bread; top it with the sour cream mixture, cucumber, and salmon; and garnish with the roe.

1/2 cup sour cream

1/4 teaspoon wasabi powder

1 teaspoon salt

1 teaspoon freshly ground pepper

12 very thin slices white bread, crusts removed

1 English cucumber, peeled and sliced into thin rounds

12 paper-thin slices smoked salmon

In a small bowl, mix the sour cream, wasabi powder, salt, and pepper, blending to incorporate the wasabi powder completely. Spread the sour cream mixture onto all 12 slices of bread; top 6 slices with cucumber rounds and 6 with smoked salmon. Close the sandwiches, cut into quarters, and serve.

Makes 24 sandwiches

Thai Tuna Rolls

These spicy little tea-style sandwiches are great for an afternoon affair with sour cocktails. Don't skip the step of heating the tortillas; it takes just a minute and makes a huge difference.

> *1 (12-ounce) can white tuna packed in water, drained*
>
> *1 tablespoon unsweetened coconut milk*
>
> *1 tablespoon Thai red curry paste (see Resources, page 95)*
>
> *1 clove garlic, finely chopped*
>
> *$1/_2$ inch fresh ginger, peeled and finely chopped*
>
> *1 green onion, white and green parts, chopped*
>
> *Juice of 1 lime*
>
> *$1/_2$ serrano chile, seeded and finely diced*
>
> *$1/_4$ cup cilantro leaves, chopped*
>
> *2 tablespoons mayonnaise*
>
> *Salt*
>
> *Freshly ground pepper*
>
> *6 (6-inch) flour tortillas*
>
> *6 leaves butter lettuce*
>
> *12 large leaves basil*

Put the first 10 ingredients (tuna through mayonnaise) in a large mixing bowl and mix until well blended. Season to taste with salt and pepper.

Warm the tortillas one at a time in a dry frying pan over medium-high heat, until they are speckled with little brown toasted marks. Remove from heat. Place 1 lettuce leaf and 2 basil leaves on each tortilla. Put 2 heaping tablespoons of the tuna mixture in the center of each tortilla and roll like a burrito.

Trim the ends of the tortillas so the filling shows; discard the tortilla ends. Slice each roll on the bias, so they look like sushi pieces. For dainty tea sandwiches, cut into $1^1/_2$-inch pieces; for a heartier sandwich, cut in half.

Serves 6 (tea sandwiches) or 12 (hors d'oeuvres)

Jalapeño Rice Cakes

These mild rice cakes are versatile and are a nice complement to a spicy dish. Try serving them with various toppings, such as Ginger Salmon Ceviche (page 85) or Spicy Mango-Apricot Sauce (page 89) and a sprinkling of sesame seeds.

1 cup jasmine or basmati rice

2 cups water

Pinch of saffron threads

$^1/_2$ cup frozen corn kernels

1 small jalapeño chile, seeded, stem removed, and finely diced

Salt

Freshly ground pepper

3 large eggs

$^1/_4$ cup half-and-half

1 teaspoon baking powder

$^1/_2$ cup yellow cornmeal

$^1/_3$ cup vegetable oil

In a medium pot, bring the rice to a boil with the water, saffron, corn kernels, jalapeño, and salt and pepper. Reduce heat to a low simmer and cook, covered, until water is absorbed, about 20 minutes.

When the rice has finished cooking, turn it out onto a baking sheet and allow it to cool until you can touch it comfortably. In a mixing bowl, whisk 2 of the eggs with the half-and-half and baking powder. Add rice and stir to combine.

Form $^1/_4$ cups of the rice into $^1/_2$-inch-thick cakes and put them onto another baking sheet. In a medium bowl, whisk the remaining egg, and put the cornmeal on a plate. After you have made the rice cakes, dip each cake all around in the beaten egg and then dust both sides with the cornmeal.

Line a plate with paper towels to drain the rice cakes, and set it beside the stove. Heat the vegetable oil in a 9-inch skillet over medium heat. When oil is 350°, add 4 cakes and cook until golden brown, approximately 4 to 6 minutes on each side. Remove the browned cakes to the paper-lined plate and brown the next batch of 4 cakes.

To keep the cakes warm while the others are cooking, place them in a 250° oven. Or set them aside and reheat them in a low 250° oven just before serving.

Makes about 12 cakes

Shrimp Toasts

When you read this recipe, you might think, What the heck is this? The whole thing is fried! But I guarantee that your guests will love it. When catering, Nancy Thomas finds that Shrimp Toasts are her most-requested appetizer. The flavors of ginger, shrimp, and green onions are bright and refreshing, and the sesame seeds add a wonderful nuttiness. These toasts are great for a cocktail party; they also make a delicious accompaniment to soup. When you fry the toasts, it is important to make sure that the oil is hot enough, because the idea is to dry cook the toast so only the surface becomes cooked and crispy. If the oil is not hot enough, the toasts will simply absorb the oil until they're cooked, and the result will be greasy and unappealing.

> 8 ounces raw shrimp, cleaned, shelled, and with tails
>   removed
> $^1/_2$ inch fresh ginger, peeled and chopped
> 1 green onion, white and green parts, chopped (about 2
>   teaspoons)
> 1 clove garlic, minced
> 1 teaspoon soy sauce
> 2 teaspoons freshly squeezed lime juice
> 1 teaspoon sesame oil
> 1 teaspoon rice vinegar
> 1 serrano chile, seeded and minced
> 12 cocktail breads (see note)
> $^1/_4$ cup white sesame seeds
> 1 $^1/_2$ cups canola oil

Put the first 9 ingredients (shrimp through chile) in a food processor and pulse until minced. (If you do not have a food processor, chop the ingredients together until very finely minced.) Spread 2 tablespoons of the shrimp mixture on each cocktail bread and sprinkle 1 teaspoon of white sesame seeds on top of each.

Line a plate with paper towels to drain the toasts and set it beside the stove. In a 12-inch frying pan, heat the canola oil to 350°. Fry the toasts in batches for 3 to 5 minutes, until the bread is golden brown and the shrimp is pink. Set the toasts on the paper towel–lined plate. Slice the toasts diagonally, and serve hot!

Makes 24 half toasts

NOTE: Square cocktail breads are sold in the deli section at most grocery stores. They are a great item to have around the house, as they provide many possibilities for creating simple hors d'oeuvres for a dinner or party.

Curry Puffs

Serve these tasty appetizers with Spicy Mango-Apricot Sauce (page 89), Mint Mojo (page 91), or Cilantro-Coconut Sauce (page 90). The puffs can be made up to two weeks in advance and frozen; to avoid sticking, separate each layer of puffs with plastic wrap and don't stack them on top of one another.

> 2 teaspoons minced onion
>
> 1 clove garlic, minced
>
> 1 teaspoon chopped green onion, white and green parts
>
> 1 teaspoon freshly squeezed lime juice
>
> 4 ounces ground pork
>
> 4 ounces ground raw shrimp (about 12 large shrimp)
>
> 2 teaspoons curry powder
>
> 2 tablespoons minced pineapple
>
> 1 teaspoon chopped cilantro
>
> 1 teaspoon minced green, yellow, or red bell pepper
>
> Salt
>
> Freshly ground pepper
>
> 1 egg
>
> 1 teaspoon water
>
> 24 wonton wrappers (see note)
>
> Canola oil for frying

Put the first 10 ingredients (onion through bell pepper) in a food processor, season with salt and pepper, and blend until almost a paste, but with colorful pieces still visible.

In a small bowl, whisk together the egg and water. Brush one side of each wonton wrapper with the egg wash and place 1 teaspoon of filling onto the wrapper. Fold over to make a triangle and pinch sides closed.

Line a plate with paper towels to drain the puffs and set it beside the stove. Heat ½ inch of canola oil in a skillet over medium-high heat until it reaches 350°. Working in batches, fry the puffs until golden brown, approximately 2 to 3 minutes each side. Drain on the paper towel-lined plate. Serve hot.

Makes 24 puffs

NOTE: As you work, keep the wonton wrappers under a lightly moistened kitchen towel, or they will dry out.

Cucumber–Mint Salad

This refreshing salad is fast to make, and it's wonderful served as an accompaniment to tea sandwiches or as a first course.

4 cucumbers, peeled and sliced
15 mint leaves, cut in a chiffonade
2 green onions, white and green parts, chopped
1 1/2 tablespoons Honteri or mirin (see note)
2 tablespoons rice wine vinegar
Salt
Freshly ground white pepper

Combine the first 5 ingredients in a medium bowl, season with salt and pepper, and mix. Allow to sit for 10 minutes to let flavors mingle before serving.

Serves 6

NOTE: Honteri or mirin is sold at health food and Asian grocery stores. I've also seen a brand called "Mirin 100% Natural Sweet Cooking Seasoning."

Hoisin Barbecue Beef

This outdoorsy grilled dish can be served whole as an entrée or cut into strips and rolled in lettuce, as an appetizer (which is how the Koreans serve it, and how it's presented here). If you use wooden or bamboo skewers, soak them for at least 20 minutes first, so they don't burn.

MARINADE

 4 tablespoons hoisin sauce
 2 tablespoons ketchup
 $1/2$ inch fresh ginger, peeled and minced
 2 cloves garlic, minced
 2 tablespoons freshly squeezed lime juice
 1 teaspoon ground cumin
 1 teaspoon chile powder
 1 teaspoon ground coriander

 12 ounces sirloin, sliced against the grain into 24 strips
 24 leaves butter lettuce
 24 lime wedges for garnish

Mix the marinade ingredients together. Set aside $1/4$ of the marinade to use as a glaze. Marinate the sirloin in the remaining marinade for 30 minutes to 2 hours. Meanwhile, prepare the grill. Remove the meat from the marinade and discard the marinade. Thread the meat on skewers and grill over very high heat for 4 to 5 minutes on each side. (If you cook the steak without cutting it, it will take 5 to 6 minutes for each side.) Remove skewers from the grill and brush with the reserved glaze. If you're waiting for other dishes to finish, you can keep the skewers warm in a 250° oven. To serve, roll each slice in a lettuce leaf, and garnish with the lime wedges.

Makes 24

Guava-Glazed Cocktail Ribs

The fruity, sour flavor of this glaze comes from the guava. This recipe is fast and easy to prepare and delicious to eat!

MARINADE

- $^1/_2$ cup guava purée (see page 21)
- 2 tablespoons rice wine vinegar
- $^3/_4$ inch fresh ginger, peeled and finely minced
- 1 clove garlic, chopped
- 1 teaspoon chopped cilantro
- 2 tablespoons pomegranate molasses (see note)

- 1 pound country-style boneless rib pork loin, sliced

In a large bowl, combine marinade ingredients. Divide mixture in half and set half aside in the refrigerator. Marinate the pork, refrigerated, in the remaining marinade for 2 to 24 hours.

Preheat the oven to 400°. Remove the pork from the marinade and discard the marinade. Wrap the pork in plastic wrap (use a microwaveable brand that doesn't melt) and then in aluminum foil and place it in a roasting pan.

Cook in the oven for 20 minutes. Meanwhile, prepare the grill. Remove the pork from the oven and allow to cool, then remove the wrapping. Cook on the grill for 2 to 3 minutes on each side to add flavor. (If you don't have a grill, a grill pan on the stovetop works well also.) Put the reserved half of the marinade in a pan over medium heat and reduce until syrupy, about 5 to 7 minutes. Brush it over the roasted pork while still the pork is still hot, and serve.

Serves 4 as an entrée, 6 as an appetizer

NOTE: Pomegranate molasses is a sweet and sour syrup available in ethnic and gourmet markets.

Ginger Salmon Ceviche

This ceviche can be served on tortilla chips as an hors d'oeuvre. Or serve a heaping spoonful on a bed of water-cress or lettuce and garnish with lime wedges as an appetizer. The ceviche will keep in the refrigerator for up to four hours. You'll know the salmon is "cooked" when it changes color to a softer, lighter pink.

> 1 pound salmon
>
> 1 inch fresh ginger, peeled and chopped
>
> 1 to 2 cloves garlic, minced
>
> 1 tablespoon minced cilantro
>
> 2 1/2 tablespoons freshly squeezed lime juice
>
> 1 tablespoon Honteri or mirin (see page 81)
>
> 1 tablespoon canola oil
>
> Salt
>
> Freshly ground pepper
>
> 1 bunch watercress or butter lettuce (optional)
>
> 8 lime wedges for garnish (optional)
>
> 36 tortilla chips (optional)

If serving as an appetizer, cut the salmon into 32 pieces; if serving as an hors d'oeuvre on chips, chop it into smaller pieces. In a medium bowl, combine the ginger, garlic, cilantro, lime juice, Honteri, and oil; season with salt and pepper; and mix. Add the salmon, coating it with the marinade. Cover and refrigerate for 30 minutes.

Makes 36 hors d'oeuvres; serves 8 as an appetizer

Kona Coffee– Black Pepper Glazed Drumettes

This delicious glaze emphasizes the flavors of molasses and coffee; cracked black pepper and coffee are also great flavors together. Be careful with the reduction; it happens fast, and if you leave the glaze on the heat too long it will be bitter in the finished dish. If you sample the reduction, you'll find the coffee taste is bitter and think you're doing something wrong–but you're not. The flavors all come together beautifully in the end.

GLAZE

   2 cups brewed Kona coffee or other dark, rich coffee

   2 tablespoons light molasses

   1 clove garlic, minced

   $1/4$ inch fresh ginger, peeled and chopped

   1 serrano chile, seeded and finely chopped

   $1/2$ cup dark rum

   2 tablespoons honey

   24 chicken drumettes (see note)

   Salt

   Freshly ground black pepper

Combine the coffee, molasses, garlic, ginger, chile, and rum in a small sauté pan over medium heat. Reduce mixture to a syrup, until it coats the back of a spoon, about 6 to 8 minutes. Remove the syrup promptly from the heat (or else you'll have burnt coffee) and stir in the honey. Set aside.

Preheat the oven to 400°. Spray a baking sheet with cooking spray. Rinse and dry the drumettes, set them on the prepared baking sheet, and sprinkle with salt and pepper. Roast until the skin is crispy, about 12 to 15 minutes. Remove from the oven and, while still hot, toss the drumettes in the glaze mixture to coat lightly. Add a generous amount of freshly ground pepper and a little salt to taste.

Makes 24 drumettes

NOTE: Chicken drumettes can be purchased frozen in most supermarkets.

Spicy Peanut Dipping Sauce

This sauce is quick and easy to prepare, and it goes well with Chicken Satay (page 64). It can be made a day ahead and reheated (for maximum flavor) just before serving.

> $^{1}/_{2}$ cup roasted unsalted peanuts
>
> 2 tablespoons peanut oil
>
> 1 shallot, chopped fine
>
> 1 tablespoon medium-hot Indian-style curry paste (see Resources, page 95)
>
> 1 cup unsweetened coconut milk
>
> 1 tablespoon soy sauce
>
> 1 $^{1}/_{2}$ teaspoons garlic-chile paste (sold at Asian food stores; see Resources, page 95)

Put the peanuts in a food processor and pulse until chopped fine, about 40 seconds; be careful not to turn them into a paste. (If you don't have a food processor, you can chop them with a knife.)

Heat the peanut oil in a 9-inch sauté pan over medium heat. Add the shallot and cook until translucent, about 2 to 3 minutes. Whisk in the curry paste, then quickly add the coconut milk, soy sauce, and garlic-chile paste. Remove from the heat and stir in the chopped peanuts. Serve warm.

Makes 1 cup

Spicy Mango– Apricot Sauce

The subtle zip in this sauce comes from the jalapeños; add more than one chile for a spicier sauce. A pretty golden peach color, this sauce is delicious with Jalapeño Rice Cakes (page 76), Chicken Satay (page 64), Curry Puffs (page 80), or grilled shrimp.

1 cup apricot purée

¹/₂ cup mango purée

¹/₄ inch fresh ginger, peeled and chopped

1 clove garlic, peeled

¹/₂ vidalia onion, chopped

¹/₄ cup fresh pineapple chunks

1 jalapeño chile, seeded and chopped

Juice of 1 lime

Salt

Combine the first 8 ingredients (apricot purée through lime juice) in a food processor and process for 4 to 5 minutes, until smooth. Season with salt to taste.

Makes 2 cups

NOTE: Apricot purée is available in gourmet and specialty food shops. To make your own, peel and pit 4 fresh apricots and purée them in your food processor. Mango purée is similarly available in gourmet and specialty food shops, or you can buy a ripe mango, peel it and cut its flesh away from the pit, and purée it.

Cilantro-Coconut Sauce

Great with Curry Puffs (page 80) or grilled poultry or fish, this is one of those terrific sauces that I can't get enough of. It will keep refrigerated for three days.

> $^1/_2$ cup shredded fresh coconut or packaged unsweetened coconut
>
> 2 serrano chiles, seeded and chopped
>
> 1 $^1/_2$ cups packed cilantro, including stems
>
> 3 green onions, white and half the green parts, chopped
>
> $^1/_2$ cup unsweetened coconut milk
>
> Juice of $^1/_2$ lemon, strained
>
> 1 teaspoon salt
>
> 1 teaspoon sugar

Combine all ingredients in a food processor or blender and purée for 5 minutes. Sauce will be thick.

Makes 1 cup

Mint Mojo

This is a tasty dipping sauce for Curry Puffs (page 80), as well as for other fried dishes. The sauce can be made a night ahead; just cover and refrigerate it. Organic spearmint has the best flavor; do not substitute peppermint in this recipe.

> 1 cup fresh spearmint leaves
> 1 clove garlic
> $^1/_2$ inch fresh ginger, peeled and chopped
> $^1/_4$ vidalia onion, chopped
> 1 green onion, white part and a bit of the green, chopped
> Juice of $^1/_2$ lime
> $^1/_4$ cup mango chunks
> 1 tablespoon honey
> Salt

Combine all the ingredients except the salt in a food processor and purée approximately 4 to 5 minutes. Sauce will be thick. If big chunks persist, add up to a tablespoon of water and continue blending. Add salt to taste.

Makes 1 $^1/_2$ cups

Menu Suggestions

SUMMER AFTERNOON SOCIAL

Seafoam (page 19)
Mary Ann and Ginger (page 20)
Shark's Tooth (page 22)

Lemon and Watercress Tea Sandwiches (page 73)
Cucumber and Smoked Salmon Cocktail Sandwiches
(page 74)
Thai Tuna Rolls (page 75)
Cucumber-Mint Salad (page 81)

COOKOUT OR LUAU

Painkiller (page 29)
Tall Blue Drink (page 32)
Nancy's Grass Skirt (page 35)
Tahitian Sunset (page 36)
Passion Fizz (page 46)

Chicken Satay with Spicy Peanut Dipping Sauce
(pages 64 and 88)
Maui Gazpacho (page 70)
Macadamia Soba Noodles (page 71)
Cucumber-Mint Salad (page 81)
Hoisin Barbecue Beef (page 82)

COCKTAIL PARTY

Coco-Nut (page 34)
Hawaii Five-0 (page 38)
Mahukona (page 39)

Thai Curry Spring Rolls (page 66)
Jalapeño Rice Cakes with Mint Mojo (pages 76 and 91)
Shrimp Toasts (page 78)
Curry Puffs with Cilantro-Coconut Sauce (pages 80 and 90)
Kona Coffee–Black Pepper Glazed Drumettes
(page 86)

Drink Suggestions for Any Occasion

FRUITY DRINKS

Mary Ann and Ginger (page 20)
Tropical Moment (page 30)
Hibiscus (page 33)
Tahitian Sunset (page 36)
Hawaii Five-O (page 38)
Passion Fizz (page 46)
Singapore Sling (page 55)

SOUR DRINKS

Seafoam (page 19)
Tall Blue Drink (page 32)
Nancy's Grass Skirt (page 35)
Mahukona (page 39)
Short Hoist (page 42)

COCONUT-WOODY DRINKS

Shark's Tooth (page 22)
Walk the Plank (page 27)
After Midnight (page 28)
Painkiller (page 29)
Kon-Tiki (page 34)
Coco-Nut (page 34)

Resources

INGREDIENTS

ASIAN FOODS
877-902-0841
www.asiafoods.com
*Ponzu sauce, chiankiang vinegar, Honteri, mirin,
Tuong Ot Toi Viet'nam.*

DAVINCI GOURMET
7224 1st Avenue South
Seattle, WA 98108
877-279-7091
www.davincigourmet.com
Various syrups, including coconut.

DEAN & DELUCA
877-826-9246
www.deandeluca.com
*Coconut syrup, Belvoir Line and Lemongrass
Cordial, Belvoir Gin Cordial. NOTE: Their stores
(in Manhattan; Washington, D.C.; St. Helena,
California; and elsewhere) have a greater selection
than what is available online.*

DOROTHY MCNETT'S PLACE
243 Sixth Street, Suite 100
Hollister, CA 95023
831-637-6444
Mango purée, papaya purée, orgeat syrup.

IMPORT FOOD
888-618-8424
www.importfood.com
*Green curry paste, red curry paste, chili paste,
hoisin sauce, kaffir lime leaves, tamarind paste,
garlic-chili paste.*

ISLAND GIFT SHOP

www.alohafriends.com

Fresh flowers, leis, coconut and passionfruit syrups, hula supplies.

MINISTRY OF RUM

www.ministryofrum.com

An excellent Web site that will help you locate specific rums.

SHOP HAWAII BY MAIL

P.O. Box 609
Kaneohe, HI 96744
808-247-3755
www.plantet-hawaii.com

Hula girl and boy salt shakers, floating flower candles, coconut and guava syrups, leis, sarongs, hula lesson videos.

TRADER VIC'S

877-7-MAI-TAI
www.tradervics.com

Location of 17 restaurants, drink mixes, orgeat syrup, passionfruit syrup.

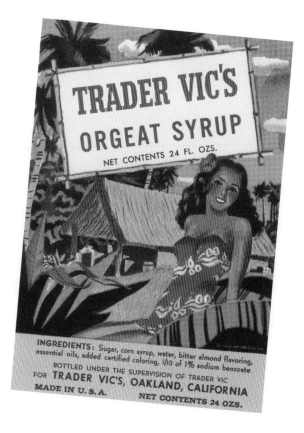

TIKI & POLYNESIAN POP OBJECTS

BOSKO
P.O. Box 300024
Escondido, CA 92030
760-807-1745
www.tikibosko.com
*Tiki and Polynesian props, including luau kits, masks,
mugs, bar supplies. (Bosko designed and outfitted the
Taboo Cove Bar at The Venetian in Las Vegas.)*

EZIBA
888-404-5108
www.eziba.com
Handcrafted objects from around the globe.

ISLAND MADNESS
800-248-0645
www.islandmadness.com
*Bar accessories, mugs, party lights, lamps,
parrot paraphernalia, aloha shirts, grass skirts.*

MUNKTIKI
591 Redwood Avenue
Sand City, CA 93955
831-393-0524
www.munktiki.com
Bizarre tiki mugs.

MYRIAH'S POLYNESIAN BAZAAR
P.O. Box 1029
Royse City, TX 75189
972-853-0621
www.myriahs.com
Wiggle dolls, music, tiki mugs, hula supplies.

ORIENTAL TRADING COMPANY
P.O. Box 2554
Omaha, NE 68103
800-228-2269 (for catalog)
*A great source for cheap paper parasols, grass skirts,
and other party accessories.*

SKIDOO
38 Eagle Street
North Adams, MA 01247
413-664-8007
Vintage aloha shirts, Hawaiian fabric, Polynesian props.

TIKI TRADER'S HAWAIIAN SHOP
1751 East Main Street
Ventura, CA 93001
805-643-8454
www.tikitrader.com
Bamboo furniture, Polynesian pop, fabric, tikis, hula girl lamps, tiki art, tiki car decals, rare Trader Vic's restaurant artifacts from the 1960s.

COCKTAIL SHAKERS (Online Sources)

BAR ACCENTS
www.baraccent.com

CATALOG CITY
www.catalogcity.com

EBAY
www.ebay.com
Many vintage and eccentric cocktail shakers.

SURPRISE
www.surprise.com

WONDERFULLY WACKY
www.wonderfullywacky.com

JENNIFER TRAINER
THOMPSON AND
NANCY THOMAS
FIND INSPIRATION.

Further Reading

Beachbum Berry's Grog Log by Jeff Berry and Annene Kaye, published in 1998 by SLG Publishing. A collection of tropical drink recipes from the 1940s, 1950s, and 1960s in a spiral-bound volume.

The Book of Tiki by Sven A. Kirsten, published in 2000 by Taschen. A fascinating, scholarly account of the "cult of Polynesian pop" in 1950s America.

Roadside Peek
www.roadsidepeek.com
An online guide to roadside tiki icons, coffee shops, motels, etc.

Tiki News
1349 Preston Way
Venice, CA 90291
www.tikinews.com
This tiki culture fanzine is a good source for information on the burgeoning tiki-revival cult and the last of the Polynesian lounges.

Trader Vic's Book of Food and Drink
Although this book is not technically out of print, it's "unavailable." But you can find copies at secondhand shops and online.

Tiki Calendar
For a copy of my
tiki calendar, contact:
Ronnie Sellers
Productions
P.O. Box 818
Portland, ME 04104
800-625-3386

Index

· A ·

After Midnight, 28
Almond syrup, 36
Antoni, Brian, 59
Appetizers, 63–91
Apricot Sauce, Spicy Mango-, 89

· B ·

Beaumont-Gantt, Ernest, 3–4, 51
Beef
    Hoisin Barbecue Beef, 82
    Tamarind-Glazed Beef,
       68–69
Bergeron, Victor, 4–5, 10, 39,
      44–45
Black Pepper Glazed
      Drumettes, Kona
      Coffee-, 86–87
Blue Hawaiian, 48
Blue Lagoon, 58
British Virgin Islands, 29
Buffett, Jimmy, 6, 11

· C ·

Cairo, Egypt, 61
Caramel syrup. See sugar syrup
Ceviche, Ginger Salmon, 85
Chicken
    Chicken Satay, 64–65
    Kona Coffee-Black Pepper
      Glazed Drumettes,
      86–87
Cilantro-Coconut Sauce, 90
Cocktail Ribs, Guava-Glazed, 83
Cocktails, 17–61
    frozen, 13, 19–22
    garnishing tips, 23, 36, 48, 56
    party suggestions, 93, 94
    preparation tips, 12–13

Cocktail Sandwiches, Cucumber
    and Smoked Salmon, 74
Cocktail shakers, 12–13, 38, 98
Coco-Nut, 34
Coconut milk
    Chicken Satay, 65
    Cilantro-Coconut Sauce, 90
    Great White, 24
    Shark's Tooth, 22
    Spicy Peanut Dipping Sauce,
      88
    Thai Tuna Rolls, 75
Coconut syrup
    Kon-Tiki, 34–35
    Painkiller, 29
    Shark's Tooth, 22
    Tall Blue Drink, 32
Coconut, toasted, 70–71
Conversions, 15
Cordials
    Ginger, 21
    Lime and lemongrass, 35
Cranberry juice
    Mary Ann and Ginger, 20
    Red Skies at Night...Sailor's
      Delight, 26
Cream, 19
Cucumber
    Cucumber and Smoked
      Salmon Cocktail Sand-
      wiches, 74
    Cucumber-Mint Salad, 81
    Maui Gazpacho, 70
Curaçao
    Blue Hawaiian, 48
    Blue Lagoon, 58
    Mai Tai Mix, 45
    Seafoam, 19
    Short Hoist, 42
    Tall Blue Drink, 32
Curry Puffs, 80–81

· D ·

Decorating tips, 21
Donn Beach. *See* Beaumont-
        Gantt, Ernest
Don the Beachcomber, 3–4,
        10, 36
Drink suggestions, 94
Drumettes, Kona Coffee-Black
        Pepper Glazed, 86–87
Duffy's Love Shack, 41

· E, F ·

Eck, Franklin, 44
Frozen cocktails, 13, 19–22
Fruity drinks, 94

· G ·

Gazpacho, Maui, 70
Great White, 24
Grenadine
        Hibiscus, 33
        Mary Ann and Ginger, 20
        Paradise Overdose, 59
        Singapore Sling, 55
        Tahitian Sunset, 36
        Zombie, 51
Guava purée, 21
        Guava-Glazed Cocktail Ribs,
                83
        Hibiscus, 33
        Mary Ann and Ginger, 20

· H ·

Half-and-half, 19
Hawaii Five-O, 38
Hibiscus, 33
Hinky Dinks, 4
Hoisin Barbecue Beef, 82
Honteri. *See* Mirin
Hurricane, 47

· I, J ·

Ice, 12–13
Jalapeño Rice Cakes, 76–77

· K ·

Kahlúa
        After Midnight, 28
        Coco-Nut, 34
        Walk the Plank, 27

Kauai, 38
Kona Coffee-Black Pepper
        Glazed Drumettes,
        86–87
Kon-Tiki, 34–35

· L ·

Leis, 23, 69
Lemon and Watercress Tea
        Sandwiches, 73
Lemon juice
        Cilantro-Coconut Sauce, 90
        Hawaii Five-O, 38
        Hibiscus, 33
        Mahukona, 39
        Seafoam, 19
        Singapore Sling, 55
        Tropical Itch, 56
Lillet, 33
Lime juice
        Blue Lagoon, 58
        Chicken Satay, 65
        Curry Puffs, 80–81
        Ginger Salmon Ceviche, 85
        Hawaii Five-O, 38
        Hoisin Barbecue Beef, 82
        Hurricane, 47
        Mai Tai, 44
        Mint Mojo, 91
        Missionary's Downfall, 52
        Nancy's Grass Skirt, 35
        Paradise Overdose, 59
        A Passionate Kiss, 41
        Shark's Tooth, 22
        Short Hoist, 42
        Shrimp Toasts, 78
        Spicy Mango-Apricot Sauce,
                89
        Suffering Bastard, 61
        Zombie, 51
Lime leaves, kaffir, 66
Luau, 69, 93

· M ·

Macadamia Soba Noodles, 71
Mahukona, 39
Mai Tai, 44
Mai Tai Mix, 45
Mango
        Hawaii Five-O, 38

Mango, *continued*
  Mint Mojo, 91
  Spicy Mango-Apricot Sauce, 89
Mary Ann and Ginger, 20
Maui Gazpacho, 70
Menu suggestions, 93
Midori
  Seafoam, 19
  Tropical Moment, 30
Mint Mojo, 91
Mint Salad, Cucumber-, 81
Mirin, 81
Missionary's Downfall, 52

· N ·

Nancy's Grass Skirt, 35
New Orleans, 47

· O ·

Orange juice
  Hawaii Five-O, 38
  Painkiller, 29
  Tahitian Sunset, 36
Orgeat syrup. *See* Almond syrup

· P ·

Painkiller, 29
Paradise Overdose, 59
Passionfruit
  Hurricane, 47
  Paradise Overdose, 59
  A Passionate Kiss, 41
  Passion Fizz, 46
  Tropical Itch, 56
  Zombie, 51
Pat O'Brien's, 47
Peanut Dipping Sauce, Spicy, 88
Pineapple
  Curry Puffs, 80–81
  Maui Gazpacho, 70
  Missionary's Downfall, 52
  Spicy Mango-Apricot Sauce, 89
Pineapple juice
  Blue Hawaiian, 48
  Mahukona, 39
  Mary Ann and Ginger, 20
  Painkiller, 29

Shark's Tooth, 22
Tahitian Sunset, 36
Tall Blue Drink, 32
Tropical Itch, 56
Tropical Moment, 30
Zombie, 51
Polynesian drinks, history, 3–4, 8–9
Pomegranate molasses, 83
Ponzu sauce, 66
Pork
  Curry Puffs, 80–81
  Guava-Glazed Cocktail Ribs, 83
  Thai Curry Spring Rolls, 66–67
Puffs, Curry, 80–81

· R ·

Raffles Hotel, 55
Red Hook, 41
Red Skies at Night...Sailor's Delight, 26
Resources, 95–98
Ribs, Guava-Glazed Cocktail, 83
Rice Cakes, Jalapeño, 76–77
Rock candy syrup. *See* Sugar syrup
Rum, 9
  After Midnight, 28
  Blue Hawaiian, 48
  Coco-Nut, 34
  Great White, 24
  Hawaii Five-O, 38
  Hibiscus, 33
  Hurricane, 47
  Kona Coffee-Black Pepper Glazed Drumettes, 86–87
  Kon-Tiki, 34–35
  Mahukona, 39
  Mai Tai, 44
  Mary Ann and Ginger, 20
  Missionary's Downfall, 52
  Nancy's Grass Skirt, 35
  Painkiller, 29
  Paradise Overdose, 59
  A Passionate Kiss, 41
  Passion Fizz, 46

Red Skies at Night...Sailor's Delight, 26
Seafoam, 19
Shark's Tooth, 22
Short Hoist, 42
Tahitian Sunset, 36
Tall Blue Drink, 32
Tamarind-Glazed Beef, 68–69
tasting, 15
Tropical Itch, 56
Tropical Moment, 30
varieties, 14–15
Walk the Plank, 27
Zombie, 51

· S ·

Salad, Cucumber-Mint, 81
Salmon Ceviche, Ginger, 85
Sandwiches
    Cucumber and Smoked Salmon Cocktail Sandwiches, 74
    Lemon and Watercress Tea Sandwiches, 73
    Thai Tuna Rolls, 75
Satay, Chicken, 64–65
Sauces
    Cilantro-Coconut Sauce, 90
    Mint Mojo, 91
    Ponzu sauce, 66
    Spicy Mango-Apricot Sauce, 89
    Spicy Peanut Dipping Sauce, 88
Seafoam, 19
Shark's Tooth, 22
Shepheard's Hotel, 61
Short Hoist, 42
Shrimp
    Curry Puffs, 80–81
    Shrimp Toasts, 78–79
Simple syrup. See Sugar syrup
Singapore Sling, 55
Smoked Salmon Cocktail Sandwiches, Cucumber and, 74

Soba Noodles, Macadamia, 71
Sour drinks, 94
Sour mix, 23
Spicy Mango-Apricot Sauce, 89
Spicy Peanut Dipping Sauce, 88
Spring Rolls, Thai Curry, 66–67
Stewart, Martha, 6, 11
St. Thomas, 41
Suffering Bastard, 61
Sugar syrup, 52

· T ·

Tahitian Sunset, 36
Tall Blue Drink, 32
Tamarind paste, 65
Tea Sandwiches, Lemon and Watercress, 73
Thai Curry Spring Rolls, 66–67
Thai Tuna Rolls, 75
Tiki Pop
    history, 2–11
    resources, 97–98
Toasts, Shrimp, 78–79
Trader Vic's, 4, 10, 42, 44, 96
Tropical Itch, 56
Tropical Moment, 30
Tuna Rolls, Thai, 75

· V ·

Vanilla syrup, 24

· W ·

Walk the Plank, 27
Wasabi, 74
Watercress Tea Sandwiches, Lemon and, 73
Wrappers
    spring roll, 67
    wonton, 81

· Y ·

Yee, Harry K., 48, 56

· Z ·

Zombie, 10, 51

About the Author

Jennifer Trainer Thompson is an accomplished cook, a James Beard Award nominee, and author or co-author of seven cookbooks and two nonfiction books. Her articles have appeared in *the New York Times*, *Travel & Leisure*, *Diversion*, *Omni*, and *Harvard*. The owner and chef of the Jump Up & Kiss Me brand of food products and hot sauces, and prolific Ten Speed poster producer. Thompson lives with her family in rural Massachusetts.